Oh, The Wonderful Things You Could Be

Written and Illustrated

By

H.B. Scribbles

You could be an Author and write not one, not two, but a half a dozen books for kids like you.

You could be an Artist and paint a masterpiece for everyone to see and be proud that it hangs high on display at the art gallery.

You could be a Race Car Driver and make the roads all around you smoky, but best of all you can win gigantic trophies.

You could be a Police Officer and make sure the community is safe and crime free, but best of all you'll protect everyone's families.

You could be a Soldier and carry the honor and respect on your shoulders because you fight for your country and always hold your composure.

You could be a Boxer and fight for championship belts and leave a graceful legacy which is truly heartfelt.

You could be an Astronaut and fly into space and land on the Moon or the planet Mars or you can sit back in the rocket ship and explore the stars.

You could be a Magician with fancy tricks and use your talent to ignite smiles and laughter with your unique mix.

You could be a Martial Artist and be a master at many martial arts such as Judo or Kung Fu, but always remember the true spirit of the art lies within you.

You could be a Baseball Player and be the best homerun hitter or the fastest throwing pitcher.

You could be a Basketball Player and be the best three point shooter or the best all-around dunker, but remember if you want to invest to becoming the best you have to practice more than the rest.

Oh, the wonderful things you could be. There are so many more options you can explore and see, but always remember to do what truly makes you happy.

Oh, the wonderful things you could be.